NERVE SQUALL

Sylvia Legris

COACH HOUSE BOOKS

2005

Published with the assistance of the Canada Council for the Arts and the Ontario Arts Council. We also acknowledge the financial support of the Government of Ontario through the Ontario Book Publishing Tax Credit Program and the Government of Canada through the Book Publishing Industry Program (BPIDP).

LIBRARY AND ARCHIVES CANADA CATALOGUING IN PUBLICATION

Legris, Sylvia
Nerve squall / Sylvia Legris. — 1ST ed.

Poems.
ISBN 1-55245-160-7

I. Title.

PS8573.E46175N47 2005   c811'.54   C2005-905594-4

to Manuela Dias, in memoriam

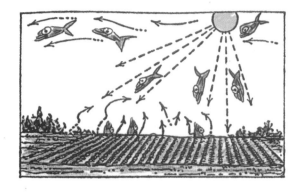

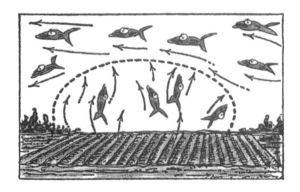

HOMUNCULI FISH VARIATIONS

BARBED

NERVE STORMS

1   GREEN BENEATH; ECCENTRIC ...

Campestre (open field): nerve-fertile, succulent (Autumn Joy, portulaca . . .). Palms prickle perplexity, electricity; senses sun-keen, idiopathic, tongue a ragged burlap of words (bramble, bristlegrass, clipped bite of mustard).

This is aura preceding storm: vein-lightning and thunder. A shock shatters a complexity of sky and miles and miles of eye-quiet and blue.

And this horizon, scattering, into intricate omen and bone (crossed fingers and knuckles knocked scared, knocked white) . . .

2   YELLOW AND FRACTIOUS . . .

Bent under fear and the sky (barbed, neuralgic) is hooked with fingers and mackerel
(the wind bristling and you, chattering, all wind chimes and teeth, threadbare nerves).

Crossing the nerve squall is crossing from eye wall to eye. A surgical edge
intersects your field of vision: below the horizon everything beyond reach, and above

brilliant — particles of eye dust, star, scotomata.

3 BLACK, MINUSCULE, A MOTE . . .

Wrapped head to foot in shadow. Nothing in the air but a slight buzz and nothing overhead but a slow plane, this sluggish sky, a sense of the unexpected. A dry place, *xerophilus*, thoughts tumbling clumps of impulse and tinder: brain embers, brain stars.

At night, a diagram of the sky is a detonation staining one side of your cerebrum
(the clock counts down meteor showers, hailstorms; small ripples of nerve and anxiety).

Sleep is a haze that leaves you mind-numb and dank, a blanket of fish scales and sleet
. . . sequin flashes, zigzag walls, ceiling constellated with angles and cuts.

4 NERVE ENDINGS, REMAINDERS; JAGGED WHITE ...

Neuro-fault line; nervequake; hemicranial. Wind rips into you — a tree split mid-trunk. Blast
of sheet-metal lightning, two plates of a skull pried apart. You are frayed optics,
mind a double edge.

The curve of your sight mimics the night as it surrounds you: dark-domed, thick-tongued
drift into sleep (you liken this to the embrace of the planetarium — ten years old every spark
igniting sky or mind, each kern or turn of exotic syllable, held a minute point of departure,
a bright speck far away,

far off in the future). Here, the moon is cut in half ... No, the whole universe is a thought
ruptured
just short of completion ...

Mute and dendritic: November. Hoary grey (*incanus*); the river twitching with ice
    and spiders,
long legs and spinning. Frenzy. You are tornado-obsessed, thoughts wild, whirling,
manic webs frosting your throat.

Around you the city is still — glacial and vapour — grey lip of the river an undefined syllable ...

Water is a pulse that melts the night into harsh beads — stinging throb of blood and temple;
inexplicable tears; lacrimation; indispensable rain ...

6 [INTERLUDE] GREY SCALE; CUMULATIVE; STRESSED MUSIC AND WATER PIXELS ...

Go away, go away ... Grey is the pitch between bright and brighter. Half-tones
  sing nervousness
(a note stringing well through another month). December, and water an approximation
of colour; collage under white, a sheath of ice over your skin.

Shiver off years' worth of cold, sore bones and teeth (the sky scored with scabbard-fish,
silver-white, ice crystals and a frozen lexicon of stars and fragments). Letters carry
  little protection;
reading and writing a distraction — of neuron and planet — forestalling doom,
  impending blizzard,
looming ice fog and sharp shards of apprehension.

Rid your arms of cold and ghosts   phantom grief; rub warmth and liniment on your limbs.
Memory of pain is a rough incrustation (a scab of storm and foreboding — the horizon blood,
a line straining your sight); and the blackest sky a soft deception, cotton batting drenched
in red. Caught between seasons; grey sky, white ice, *rain, rain* ...

Red red red red red. Raspberry (thin vein of blue); tomato (strained through
   yellow). Everywhere
red. Hands lined with fire and rage, you are fear-marked, brain-scarred, soul choppy with
rough sea and disaster.

Angor animi: imminent storm. Skies dangerous (blood draining your cheeks) and
   clouds, menacing
clusters (*cumulus congestus*), a scarlet band tightening your brow.

The night is spiked with integers: 1 *you wake* 2 *you wake* 3 *you pace and you pace and* ...
Hardwood-weary (flat-footed, languishing pine), doubled over, tree-green.

—

Morning and the sun burns orange in your heart — bile and red sky, portentous. In
   your mouth,
taste of bitter and jagged star; mind frantic with erratic planets, platelets, irregular
orbit.

Cacumenis, cauticolus (mountain crest, cliff). Roots take hold through the top of your head — *Coryphantha calipensis*, stiff-fingered and needled. Losing air and balloon-veined, tachycardic.

Upslope fog. Grappling for rope and hook. Ascent is a labour of cold words and worry.

Panting. Falling in and out of sleep. Falling: over cliff-edge and -hanger, body wrenching jerking myoclonic. Wracked with question marks and on the brink of

breath — the forecast low visibility, thick enunciation. Ineffable lungs.

INTO THE BIZARRO SQUALL

1   ST FRA

Stratus fractus; fractostratus. Cloud shreds and streamers; rain-cooled air,
     air-drenched skin.

St fra: *Holy funnel clouds!* Whole sky woven of light ribbon and tickertape; whirling
     currents and
storm dervish. Stern climate; itinerant sky; spiral down then dusting

austerity — here and here ...

—

Breaking to pieces: tooth and nail, enamel. Glass-eyed and fog. A vista of steam vision
     and vapour
(flying cows and houses

falling on witches). Stripe-socked and polka-dotted, spots before your eyes (the fear
of clouds in you — kneel to the east, kneel to the west, pray for clear sky and solid colour,

pray for small dogs).

WOOF WOOF WOOF. August is maniacal, wild dog fights, matted hair. Helixed nights
with one eye always vigilant. Restless restive. Twirling sheets, tilt-a-whirl gut.
    Irritable, irascible,
rickety with alliteration and going to Hell — definitely GOING TO HELL.

and you can't wait ...

—

Sick sick sick; sick of stink, sick of summer, godforsaken and sticky as dog. And that smell
— what in Hell's name is that smell? Vinegar! Sleep prickling with formication ...
    No not *that*.
FORMICATION: sweat dreams; hymenoptera; ants invading every orifice with larvae and acid

and the walls reek! of vinegar and old grease (cold french fries *euuu* nasal flood and food
... *dizzying dizzying* ...)

Sustenance holding the clouds in place? Bellyfuls of rain and stamina. And you
    just drifting
light and dust, contradiction, absurdity. Pulled in every direction but

unflappable sky. Pray for three hours of drowsy climate, torpid forecast, subsidence
of dog squabbles, cat scuffles, street racket traffic clatter sirens and ...

—

Foghorn: MWWAAAA MWAAA (shut up!) ... 'What why when someone tells
    me to shut up I ...'

SHUT UP! ... The night never ends your head throbbing with falling barometer
    and chickens
puddling the foot of your bed incessant clucking birds fucking like there's no tomorrow
    and the sky

this time is falling for real ...

CONVERGING POULTRY

Broody broody broody. Lingering heat bloat and preoccupied with poultry:
   Red Star, Redcap,
Rhode Island Red, Buff Orpington, Leghorn (brown, black, silver, duckwing, black-tailed).
Give these birds a leg up, but first

pray. Pray to St tr for fight-or-flight clouds, scattering feathers,
zero-chicken-tolerance and 20/20 vision

of the sun and the moon …

—

St tr: stratus translucidus. Cloud layer thinning, blind lungs give way to stable air — Pop!
in your ears and what do you see what do you hear? Music? Singing?

Ain't nobody here but us chickens … (cluck cluck cluck stuck in your head stuck in your …

5 SERIOUS SURGE

Crayfish, craw (Daddy don't choke on surprise!). Split-open sky, spitting wind, and yes
those are cows on the roof! Fish at the window!

Caught caught caught in whirlpool and drama.

—

Tide-dream. Flash-melt. Crab-spinning river — clockwise, clock-silly, your sense of season
skewered and skewed (beluga-pale, impaled in sleep, limbless and paralysis
rising like water) …

—

Cold flesh and flabby, moisture-wrinkled. *Mr. van Winkle wake up wake up*! You
    have over-
wintered, slept through too much snow and now water

water everywhere …

LIMBIC SWIM

LIMBER UP

Be nimble, be quick. O agile agile swimmer (o gold star, limbic star). O temporal
temporary tranquility.

—

Ocean reflects the longest lukewarm sky in memory; tertiary sky (rainbow washing rainbow).
Trout and mackerel are laaazy laaazy cloud formations, languorous, back-floating ...

aaahhh ...

—

Hey! *Say! what a lot of fish there are.* (Is this up? Is this down?) Sky is water water is sky
and everything
swimming swimming into one swirling pool

... nonstop grey ...

—

Nonstop yellow, nonstop red; o sunfish, o anemonefish — forget-me-not and I will plant you
in subterranean brain, prehistoric brain (prehensile roots and curling determination) ...

CUMULUS HOMUNCULI FISH FORMATION #1

FISHBLOOD SKY

1   [DEAD DRIFT]

Always an arm's length of line between you and the shore. An ocean of measure and wait,
each syllable a long-drawn lap, treading water wider and ...

Land-driven, on your fingertips an imprint of sand and on the tip of your tongue
(just the tip) buds of brine and nostalgia, sepia and silver

gelatin; and fins and scales — a fine dip-net separating inside from out (reticulated skin,
   a scar-
montage, sole a mosaic; splintered palm and touch
mediated   *by sky by*) ...

Falling fish; wounded fish; carp carp carp. Stench of cod liver and creosote.
    Everything slips
dripping from your fingers, meaning and words (grey cell by red); blood-beads enough
to string every planet the colour of Mars   (and you you would

rage if you could find your way there,

an obstacle course of broken rosary, broken

Prayer and reverie, of rock-chip of pebble.

The sun falls five times in the course of a conversation. Words rise and recede and
    your voice
is the moment before stone skips surface. Water a repetition of ever-widening intervals
(harmony of absence and lapse).

You are craggy embankment, here for the long haul, and I (clacking onyx and quartz
    for luck)

watery with superstition.

Moon aphasia; mute-eyed and tongue   a blind pool enveloping. The tide serrated
    with syntax
and hook. *Mayfly, fly-fish, flying fish*; snarl of fin and wing, spiny things

that catch; a fixation — on finger and tack, thumbscrew and nail, needle and spike and bone

spurs under your skin and above
the sky an intimidating net, dragging:

medusa head, horse head, nebula;
fingerling and eel; spotted trout, rainbow;
halo and tear …

Drop everything you know into murky sky (every question mark a nagging hook).

—

¿ Rain attack and brain

a flood of panic saturating sleep: rapid eye, rapid heart, white water and blur. Nightmares SWIM DEEP IN YOUR SKIN, BUT DAYS BEFORE ARE RESTLESS, A RESIDUE OF ORANGE PEEL AND RADIO.

(You are tuned to old smells and frequencies

in reverse; rain accruing upward; a vocabulary
of null and ...)

6

Clouds empty
then hemorrhaging
mackerel.

Fish sky and fins (mare's-tail, seahorse). Currents rise and fall (air patterning water) and
    the sky
all pulsing corpuscle and vein: impending turbulence, rain; thunder, lightning (embolism
and shock).

Embouchure — your mouth tumbling water mumbling ... stone arteries, the river slows,
    a slow
stagnation, days and years   (and years later my own

father comatose for a week, cumulus clouds repeating *one-fish-two-fish-red-and-blue*
    this rhythm
dysrhythmic, and the sky ...

Stung with jellyfish: gelatinous; paralytic and thick; quavering blood. Your voice is water-logged and tremulous; tri-barbed, triple-hooked (demisemiquaver; diminuendo

down down down).

—

Bottom-dwelling; alexia. The seabed lettered with body parts and half an alphabet; *a e i* ...
five fingers, five toes, phantom-limbed and one side of a torso, hemiplegic. Half-heart, half
in the dark ... *and many times you many times why — questions questions* ...

Foggy answers, the sky veiled
in gillnet.

Tangle of eye and tongue, tingling nerves, estranged from both saliva and skin. Backwatered, rainbow and oasis are scotoma and exhaustion mirage (backstroke, breaststroke, breathless). Your sight plays tricks, light-tics, twitches; false colour, floating eye, and half the sky,

hemianopia, half the sky missing. You are wedged

between ocean and rock, airlocked (catfish shimmer through you, ghostly memory and synaesthetic, two minds, two bodies, mammal and gills). You begin where water begins
    and end

back where you started.

In spring this mountain was a fish
— Hayden Carruth

9   [STRIKE]

Fish tales and figments; coming up for air; tighten the line. There is something on
   your hook,
you feel it.   *It's raining it's pouring*   rain rain battering down, and fish

flopping at your feet (fat feet, fin-fat), gill-deep before you know it, an overflow. And clouds,
balloon-fish and puffer, helium-happy, high-pitched high, inhaling hot air, exhaling ...

Anoxic: out of breath, giddy;
adrift ...

CUMULUS HOMUNCULI FISH FORMATION #2

CYCLONIC AND WHINNYING

1   WITHERSHINS

Divergent swimmer; paddle upright and upstream from sun and shallow *stroke stroke mis-stroke*. Whirl and whirl against the clock. Stretch out your neck, snuffle the air, let rain fill your eyes with horse clouds, sagging bellies, long-winded whinnies and grins toothy like crazy.

Bolt for shelter when you see the whites of mares' eyes, some jaundiced, some swelter-stricken, red streaking white streaking red. Stallion skies presage bloodletting and lightning ...

(Who's there? Who's there?) Hooves thundering temples the sky demanding answers: *Who are you? Where are you? What do you remember?*

—

Hovering horse, buoyant horse; equine sky and sea. Sing sing *syngnathidae*: treble clef fish, piccolo-snouted and bones tuned to bass-depth and bass.

Seagrass bed (aquatic sleep); reef pillows bulging with tiny sea skeletons and the skies

dripping pipefishdreams, pipehorse, starry morays.

Hip Hip Hip Hippocampus. Seashore memory, seahorse-sighted ...

What the seahorse saw was sinew and bone, everything on the wrong side of skin, a wide flexing muscle of sky over water — vertiginous, fearsome, every treacherous shade

of painted eel (bloodworm and fishgut), a chaos of colour: sea-whip orange, stickleback red, beluga sturgeon roe the blackest black. A morass of eggs looking like eyes and eyes like ...
                                wink wink ...

and never never any clear water and even out in the sky
                                out in the sky, no one sleeps ...

                                ——

Sea air-veined: swimbladder-heavy, bloatfish-light. Sink and rise sink and rise sink   into quagmire and back *Sea ✧ Horse ✧ See ✧ Saw* flotsam and yet ...

(What the seahorse saw played like a game of flawed squares and muddled moves knight takes old maid and queen goes fish — jumbling tiddlywink, periwinkle, pondfish, pawnfish, you feel like a prawn out of ...)

Out of air and out of water; curls that kink and cords that bind. Hysterical winds on the way and you are reeling way out of your league ... wet-footed and at least 20,000 ways to tread water: past starfish and fish-star; wave-frenetic seaweed, clamshells cli-clicking like ...

Cast a net to shore, pull sky toppling on top of you, cyclonic and whinnying, water-sputtering quarterhorse, racing, whirling, cirrus to sea — mare's head to seahorse, nebula to water haze, furious flurry to

. . . n o t . . . a s . . . c a l m . . . a s . . . c o u l d . . . b e . . .

sea and cirri (*que sera cirri*). Whatever will be will be knob-headed and spiky-at-the-mane, chameleon eyes and monkey-tailed-grasping, grasping and curling curling and

... gasp for air then plunge, headstrong and horse nostril first; fish losing air, horse losing water, and you
                    raining
                         a confusion
                                of elements
(Man-of-watery-nerves, man-of-unforeseen-storms. Headwinds, tailspins, flipping bellywhops flopping

lies that smack true and truth ...)

Sea ✧ Horse ✧ See ✧ Saw

Whatever will be the air reeks of fish oil and familiarity. Trickling dendrites and denticles,

memory rough-scaled everything grey-no-matter-what … sloughed cells, churning slough;

brain ✧ bog, seahorse ✧ bobbing, swimming in limbo …

SHIFTY WEATHER

A shifty business this, writing the poem's weather.
— Robert Kroetsch

1

Air bubbles orbit your coffee cup. Wind forever blowing the outside in: pollen, pesticide, exhaust. The weatherman, either indecisive or contemptuous (take your pick), holds out rain in the one hand and migraine in the other. O blustering succotash! O mother of lightning!

—

Weather-locked in an imminent storm pocket you are everywhichway, every channel mucky in sludge (the weatherman *definitely* dripping disdain).

CUMULUS HOMUNCULI FISH FORMATION #3

2

Expect rain:

When the calico stands on its brain.

When the retriever's tail becomes a yardstick.

When little brown bats nest under your pillow.

When groundhogs are too thunderstruck to pore over shadows.

3

Dash your buttons! Batten the hatches! Sky is black, the grass grows backwards. Rain fills your skull and fever your toes. Lose your composure and

SCARED COPROLALIC! (O muck-suckle! O muck-snipe!)

4

Take warning! Take warning! Red ants at morning and the shortest distance to a storm a panic-breeding procession. Ants fretting in linear precision. Brew of formic acid and tannin (souchong tea and the linger of forest fire). Taste the sting in the air ... *smack smack* ... blistering lungs and everywhere bugs: blackflies and ticks, chiggers and aphids (skin sticky a perpetually repellent swarm of words — gluey, mucilaginous) ...

5

Power lines oscillate with ambivalent birds. Flickflickflick *grackle, blackout* stiletto bills puncture the dark, talons

vice-grip your breath. Boomerang-veined: here a bird there a bird everywhere the same bird *now you see it now you don't ha-ha-ha-HA-ha* ... thrum up the side of your neck *thwack thwack thwack* ...

6

FLASH!-*pop* FLASH!-*pop* Your brain an erratic electricity. Failure of memory every 5000-hour light bulb waning at once. (Afraid of the dark even your Fred Flintstone nightlight lets you down ... power outage shines a spotlight on your weakness of character.)

—

Feather-shedding fear of the dark and déjà vu that same crow crashing the window again and again ... hope raining eternally wet-witted the two of you water-loony, drenched repetitive ...

7

Low-flying kites tornado you in turmoil. O crackpot sky! O thunderclap and fright!

—

Rain's sucked all the pretty worms from the ground (tiptoeing through the grass a lesson in squelch and squirm). The sun is squeamish shows itself then ...

Fickle fickle fickle ... Barely-touching-down funnel clouds, storms that never quite break. When it rains it portends change of temperament; a drop in pressure you acquiesce

— turbulence, jet stream collision ... *O the pain, the pain* ...

8

What gives?

Rivers foaming at the mouth?
Knots impossible to unknot?
Clammy stones? Clumping salt?
Walls sweating hieroglyphics?

Translate the clouds and wait ...

BIRD STORM CLOUD

ORNITHOLOGICAL TAUTOLOGIES

RAVENOUSNESS

I sing to you, almost deadly birds of the soul
— Rilke

1

Crosswise sky (black, looming, ominous). Birds flashing this way and that.

Loquacious, articulate birds (*speak-to-me-speak-to-me-speak-to-me*).
Long-winded, hot-lunged, beak-diving-barometer birds.

—

Clouds insensible with rain-hungry crows. WAW-ter WAW-ter WAW-ter
enough to quench a cyclone

of craw-parched perching birds. Light-headed. Woozy warblers.
Wobbling off-key.

2

Wake with a mouth of sand and gulls circling above you. Stumble and pitch.
The floor a heaving stomach and you green to the gullet with all the wrong feet
(feet for climbing, feet for clinging, feet for grasping prey).

Sea-leg-stumped. Thirsty as a loon.
Figments of lurching breakers and nasal squalls … KA-HONK! KA-HONK!
… pestering geese.

The water cooler sloshing like so much nausea.

3

Sea/Saw. *Sea*/Swell.
(Mean Sea Coming Unlevelled.)

Wet bulb depressed. Marred sky. Atmospheric overload.

—

See every feather through a magnifying glass — B-movie mites and dust motes
are colossal birds poised to strike (irrefutable Hell

is a daunting inkling in the corner of your eye. Demon floaters;
forked tongues and pitchfork-tailed).

4

BANG! FLASH! Brobdingnagian thunder crash. Ear-splitting decibels.
(Mutant hawks shriek through REM-storm and narcoleptic rime

    ... KEE-AHHR KEE-AHHR

        ... extend your claws, dig in your heels, *screeeeech* ...

           —

The sky spits bits of pandemonium,
while god-arrogant birds (prey-omniscient, global-warning)
condemn you
like so much run-of-the-kill carrion.

5

Cleft lightning. Quick-fire birds.
Zoom vision instinct and up-close appetite.
Rrravenous.

—

Running in your sleep. Can't-get-off-the-ground dreams.

Butcherbird-flustered (garnished to kill and nowhere to go;
sleep-paralyzed and rotisseried
in allegory   *spinning spinning*;
bed of coals, a Macintosh in your mouth
— bird-pecked-apple-apnea … *don't gag don't gag*).

6

Flat-out-sleep-broke. Bird-infuriated.
Losing ground and graceless

as a dodo.

STRANGE BIRDS; TWITCHING BIRDS

1

Holy Bone Pickers! Holy Bird Mutations! Terminal Highway just lingers and lingers — unpleasant aftertaste and *maddening* jingles in your head (*Double-your-pleasure? Double-your-pain?*). Nostrils stinging of hot rubber, Firestone-fast food ... and now what? Roadkill phantoms? Circling above you heat mirages?

No
    such
        luck.

The pluck-ugliest birds you'll ever see. Lizard-naked skulls, red-raw skin (Homely monks! who marinate in the bath too long — brush scrub and flagellation ... *Count-your-tormented-prayers, birds.*).

Opportunistic birds. Birds who strike while the flesh is still hot. Incessant pickers; nitpickers. (Wash your hands a thousand times and still

these vultures get under your skin.)

—

Pick-pick-pick-pick-pick. Crawling with buzzing things and microscopic buzzards, little beaks, little pecks. Unnerving paresthesia (epidermal pointillism): a continent's worth of peck-marks, your body a stormy rash of range-map and no relief in sight! Out-of-kilter flight paths; shaky-on-takeoff navigation. (*Migratosis neurosis?*)

OCD: Overshadowing Condor Distress. Fear of bald-headed birds.

2

O little gull, little gull (*Larus minutus*). O Bonaparte's gull. (*Hey! Keep those coverts where I can see them.*)

Little gull, Lilliputian gull. Consumed with small galling swimming birds, the tiniest things send you wet-browed and reeling (eddying out of control and the weir has never looked so good).

—

Kittiwake Kittiwake Kittiwake (*getaway-getaway-getaway*).

Thorny nerves and bird-suspended bridges. O *frigate frigate* frigatebirds — even pelicans won't look you in the eye. The sky creepy with rooks and here you are, condemned, to the wrong side of the boardwalk — *checkcheckcheckcheckcheckcheckcheck* — a never-ending game you are destined to bungle.

3

Kitchen Hell. Recipe Doom.

Lose your way in eggshells and fowl drippings. Falling-from-grace Angel Cake. Burnt-to-a-crisp Devil's Food. Bad leavening. Blood-curdling milk. And birds HARASSING HARASSING HARASSING you from stove to fridge and back.

Echolalic birds ... TEA-KETTLE TEA-KETTLE TEA-KETTLE ... Mimicking birds ... DRINK-YOUR-TEA-EE-EE-EE ...

— *they've got their nerve*! Repetitious birds! Ornithological tautologies!

—

... CHECKCHECKCHECKCHECKCHECK

Piebird, ovenbird: Off. Off. Off. Check the stove again and again. Chicken grease on the element? (CHECK) Fear of fire? (CHECK) Fear of flame? (CHECK CHECK-CHECK)

What a witches' sabbath of wings
— Robinson Jeffers

4

Little bird, little bird, LET ME OUT. *Not-a-chance Not-a-chance Forget-get-get-get-it …*

Damn this cracked crow! Damn this wicked net! A snare of ritual and vexation: Icterinæ Tyranny. Grackle Sacrament. Sins of the Feather. Banging your head till you're blackbird and blue.

All the time in Hell on your hands and an eternity of bird devotions on an endless string of millet … Ave Aviary, Ave Oriole, Hail Bob-bob-bob Bobolink …

—

Dead of night and captive to an unremitting chorus of blackbirds: Rusty Falsetto (creaking demons and doors and coming unhinged!), Nasal-Toned Tricolour (triple-glazed windows, blue-in-the-face), *Quiscalus mexicanus* … Arriba! Arriba! Arriba!

Grisly dreams. A palpitating litany of shadowy birds: *Quiscalus quiscula* (Commonest Common Grackle), *Euphagus cyanocephalus* (Brewer's Blackbird, volcanic stomach), *Euphagus* … esophagus (a nagging bird in the throat and your hands

won't stop trembling).

5

Unshakable birds! (Being followed? Being watched?) Run run but never escape the flutter of wings in your chest.

—

Demon-faced birds stare daggers from building ledges and at every corner you turn (*every corner you turn!*) ... Twitching birds (nit-crawling catastrophe carriers), Tourettic birds (*odious-odious-odious*), birds skulking in turrets (Stone-Feathered Gargoyles, your cries for help

just so much sputtering).

—

Featherless. *Hopeless!* Overwhelmed with bird urges and the compulsion to tic the compulsion to tic the compulsion ...

Are you dreaming? Are you sleeping? (*Dormez-vous? Dormez-cheep-cheep* ...)

BIRDS (AN APOCALYPTIC POEM?)

1   DEATH, JUDGEMENT, HEAVEN, HELL,/AND SPRING...

Idiocy of March! Foolish April! Nonstop birds dare you to cross a wire-crazy edge. You are raving
with rumours of sun and flower plumage: blue sky and the whole blooming
blossoming spectrum.

Instead, black battering above you *your poor grey grey grey grey dull throbbing head* ...

Migrainous birds. Pain-black grackle and crow. Out of nowhere a queasy foreboding
of jackdaws
trapped

in a ribcage. You are black-hearted, the sky funereal — priestly black and heavy-
garment-forbidding
(hyperventilate your prayers one wing beat at a time: for–give me, for–give me, I am
kuk-kuk-kuk-kuk-kuk-kuk-kuk-kuk bird–bad ...).

———

DOOMED DOOMED
to eternal bird vertigo, fluttering pulse, countless arrhythmic miscalculations:
always a beat off, always a beat short, always out of ...

Sink now or forever hold your tongue — against cold steel and deception,
    duplicitous cohorts,
a split-beaked compulsion to scream (open your mouth and all that escapes are
    mock calls and lack-
of-song birds); butcherbirds, a thick sinister execution

... *crows* ...

—

Clouds with intermittent coruscation (black delirium and flash). Dread-struck sky and
    imminent blast.
Crow-dizzy in despair, *Corvidae*-condemned ... Throw up your arms and throw
    CAW! CAW!
birds to the wind ...

Hooded gull; laughing hangman; crash of wings in the sky and your feet giving out
    beneath you.
The air sultry with thaw fervour and gallows humour. Venal equinox and desire
    springs eternally
out of reach. Flat on your back, blind-headed with season frenzy, then all those
    Hell-twisted birds

... *peck peck peck peccadilloes at the window* ... bent on temptation ...

3 BLIND MAN, BIRDMAN, BUFFLEHEAD, BLUFF...

Ha-ha-ha-ha-ha. Laughing gull just another accident on the south Saskatchewan. The
    train bridge
strung with nooses and fruitless booby traps (in the corner of your eye a fat man brandishing
    a blade
and a laugh — *hee-haw-hee haw*ing and raucous). You are humourless,

the air around you waiting to attack. Cold city, cold river, metal girders of the bridge beckon you
in frozen tongues (many have been here before you).

Trek from one length of track to the next eternal in the dark (nothing to do but lay down
    your head,
listen ... for the chug chug of blood and piston) ...

—

(*pssst pssst*) ... The night an unending mockery of hoot owls and nocturnal guffaws *killy-killy-killy*,
nerve-chillingly shrill. Morning and heads roll into corners screaming GO-BACK-GO-BACK-GO ...

It feels like a game. Hot potato hot potato musical chairs, pass GO too many times short-circuiting
... Short Line, Pennsylvania Avenue, take a ride on the Reading take the next rail-sharp turn ...

—

STEP RIGHT UP! Upstarts and redstarts (*plenty of egrets!*). World's biggest travelling
    bluebird morgue,
grosbeak, bluethroat (*blood from the jugular!*). Close the door (*cold closing-in-on-you walls!*),
count to ten (*closer closer closer!*), hold your breath ... *aah-aah-aah* ...

The calendar marred with birds and you are *kik-kik-kik*-kicking all the way into June.
180 days scratched with black X's and crow's feet: bird-of-two-minds (*goodandevil
    goodandevil*);
single-minded bird (plotting the sky).

—

♪ *birds* ♪ *notorious* ♪ *birds (* ♪ *ruffled feathers and fiendish* ♪ *)*

Rain-divining ducks; rain-murderous blackbirds, hollering hollering from sunrise to sunrise.
Long day after longest day of wing-striped sky, sun eclipsed by feathers. Blue-black,
    bruise-black,
antigen-tinged half moons under your eyes. Beleaguered just by thoughts
of countless birds, prospects of an entire summer riddled with peck-marks and quills ...

Even under closed eyes: oneiric birds; four stages of sleep, each one soaring you deeper
and deeper into raptor-psyche: Cooper's hawk, Red-tailed hawk, Black-shouldered kite
    keep-keep-keep

... getting sleepy ... sleepier ...

Seeing stars; seeing birds. Hypnotic and rapid-firing REM-sleep: Flammulated owl,
  flame-hot Lucifer
hummingbird. Steller's jay (*Cyanocitta stelleri*); Blue jay (*Cyanocitta cristata*).
  Spellbinding tidings
of magpie, Yellow-billed and Black — sleep-scavengers, foraging dream ...

Pica nuttalli; Pica pica. Wake with an appetite for danger and the allure of shiny objects
  in your eyes
— phosphenes and scintillating egg nebulae (star-blotched, star-marbled). Vascular sky
  and a stranger
in black hood and hawk-tail at the foot of the bed ...

—

Fright moult. Visceral aura. A menacing unkindness of bird phantoms. Rock wren. Redpoll.
!REDRUM ... birds flying backwards into blackest ...

Caught

in kestrel limbo;
song sparrow purgatory. The year unfolds in precarious assemblages of bad-numbered birds
(13 blackbirds, 13 rooks, 13 x 13 x 13 black vultures and buzzards); *birds birds birds birds birds*

everywhere. Birds at your feet, birds at your head, birds pulling you further and further
  from grace.
Bird-besieged; foaming at the mouth, hydrophobic and leery of hydro poles ...

Birds lurking on wires, waiting ...

AGITATED SKY ETIOLOGY

STUMPED SKY (QUESTIONS OF MISSING WEATHER AND BIRDS)

1

Typical typical typical. A recent affinity for birds and now where are they?
No wings, no leaves. Just nerves crunching underfoot.

Wrong season for pelicans and geese and now a gaggle of goosebumps
erupting omens and Braille up your skin. You are ill at ease

with interpretation. (Reading the snow for signs
does nothing to take the chill off.) Overhead,
ice-capped birds shriek *Defeat! Defeat!*

2

Lack-Lack-Lack. Lonely ducks plead for rain but rain rain's gone away and the trees
have pulled inside themselves (multi-stumped and trunks
a frazzle of missing leaves).

Weather is numb. Nonsensical. The sky all thumbs and fingers falling.
What's the point here, what's the point there: unceasing questions.

Clouds a flummox of fluster. Flux. Ice miasma. (Second nature
a temperate climate preceding storm.)

3

Snow déjà vu.
Every snowflake a thumbprint,
freeze-framed; dendrite crystals and arctic-
anæsthetized nerves.

—

Circling and circling and always arrive at the same
lack of conclusion:
What the cold feels like is …
What the cold feels like is …
What the cold feels like …

O spit-on-it spit-on-it … The cold

is always a predictable shock (a doomed man waiting for the blade to drop).
Ice-gleaming metal. Sting and
so cold you barely feel your tongue-tip your tongue
rip out of your mouth
or your limbs *Where are my legs? I can't feel my arms.*

… winter-dark and *Where's the bloody socket?*

4

Everything fades to …

Whiteout. Hypnotic and nose-close to hypothermia.
Blizzard-blinding (snow like something out of *Fargo*).
Winter a mile-high silver screen

tarnished to monotone. Unrelenting;
an eight-months' sustained
sub-zero note.

—

Look down,
look down,
look waaay down …

It's as if you were never here (you start to believe this).
Walk the same footprints every day
and every day they disappear — drowning
in the whiteness of it all, hyper-invisibly visible;
white trudging white.

5

Snow paranoia.

*Run! Run! The sky's falling! The sky's falling! The sky's
losing all sense of itself ...*

phut phut phut. Feet futility on snow.
Limbs falling everywhere (flailing arms and legs
running on the spot ...).

Night palsy. Nightmares ice-
incapacitated: disembodied snow prints, decapitated
snow angels.

—

Weather apparitions.
Glacial ghosts? Snow golems?
(Unsullied snow sticky enough to fashion limbs from.)

6

You know this climate like the shape of your hand inside your mitt;
increasing numbness (face licked with cold, ice-slick
questions on your tongue, answers
fewer than you have fingers to count on), familiarity

an avalanche
waiting ...

TRUNCATED

The cameraman has tried to make an amputee whole again …
— Yusef Komunyakaa

TRUNCATED

somewhere in the other room

———————

Bedevilled edges.
Bevelled plexus.
Phantom palimpsest.

———————

Walls flowered
in turn of the last century's hæmatoma.
Osteoporotic plaster,
bruised ceiling.

Rub down the woodwork
with clove oil and codeine.
Pain-numbing burnish.

Years trapped within a year.

Ghost
snaps, flutter
release, sweeping
second
hand
figments.

———————

Neurogenic-calendric

(facsimile of days;
book of erroneous hours).

Months are an eye-patchwork
of floaters and blind spots.

Buff and rebuff.

The wind polishes you
to granite-postured vigilance then
buffets you, eyes first — all open
membrane; the clouds
lenticular, a nictitating sun. Spring frightening up
in flits and darts, the thinnest-of-hopes-

phantom.

Wind
chill
contra-
diction: Speech migrates

to a different place in the forecast;
clouds break
over a fragile hemisphere,
intermittent fury, language fitful
with a plethora

of lack — clench your face everything's black
ice, perspicacity
dicey at best.

Ghost percussion. Strike up
the sound of one hand not clapping; strike
one solid body against another
that's left the room.

———————

Your cat who's been dead fifteen years meows
    when you shake a box of macaroni.
The excavation site down the street wails
    for leaded windows and brass.
The hospital freezer moans with unbearably itchy body parts.
An agonizing sweet tooth where there isn't a tooth
    (you crave caramels, bridgework, anaesthesia).

Torn limbic from limbic. A rift
between eye and sensation.

Adrift with no lifeline and no hands
to expose the whites
of your knuckles (in any case),
the tightrope burns
cutting a swath across your palms.

———————

Mirror duplicates; water replicas; dreaming
of prosthetic sheep:

Knife-throwing, flame-juggling,
besting Lionel Hampton on the vibraphone,

shuffling a mean deck of cards,
writing a novel with gestures instead of words.

Look ... no hands!

middle ear almanac

[Saturn
on a
backward
slide]

Turbulence.
                    Auditory
eustasy.
Glaciers shift
the narrow corridor from pharynx
to bottleneck to
eustachian-
pool. Pressure gradient

gives way to air-pop
and ricochet, antechamber

to chamber ... Trip
over suspicious membrane
— tortuous cat's cradle,
high-speed double dutch —
into an eddy

of commotion.

———————

Sonic
congestion.

Purgatorial
traffic jam: corkscrewing

countercochlearwise
the only way out.

The fall seems eternal
but the winter ...

Air cackles off-key.
Incessant tympanic
orchestral
movements frozen

[the day
will be
8 hrs.,
43 min.
long]

somewhere backwards
in time. Static-
bristling (cochlear

hoarfrost).

Ciliary. Ice haze. Ice-
lashes. Cold glass

fuzzy with lanugo. (Double-glazing embraces
the corpse of a spider, microscopic
hair mascaraed white.)

———————

Everything overstated:
crackling heat ducts,
the refrigerator cycling,
the whistle behind the newscast.

Cold storage: squirrel away
the season, cranium
packed in ice. Seal the cracks
with duck down, eiderdown, hair
panicked on end.

[Venus
conspicuously
high]

—————————

Hermetic paranoia.
Window fittings frozen inoperative.

Fenestra vestibuli.
Fenestra cochlea.

Nothing gets in (car exhaust drizzles the street,
a man shovels his walk wheezing
ice crystals and obscenities);
nothing escapes …

Echo cavern. Whirl
-winding ganglia.
Occluded auditory front. An ossuary
of sound relics
(a door slammed during the Nixon administration;
rodents in the roof four houses ago;
an argument over *The Carol Burnett Show*).

Stalactites, stalagmites
(you can never remember the difference).
Noise assails you from north and south,
drum-puncturing icicles, ossicles
petrified.

Lost in mastoid space.

Gyrating in perpetuity ear mollusc.
Cochlear discombobulation.
Minute hairs of that-which-can't-be-grasped ...

Cilia (goosebumps on your goosebumps!).
Superciliary (eyebrows balance an avalanche).
Supercilious (glacial; scornful; inundated by a racket of ice, snow-

stupefied voices).

Never a question of cold
but gradation: frazil ice,
pancake ice, pack ice.

[The Moon
hovers close
to Uranus]

The climate staggers you
into by turns ear-baring audacity
and a dread of deep-freeze decibels
(the river thaws, solidifies;

auricle prophecy and spur
-of-the-moment acoustics

thwarted
by mercury).

pyrocumulus

———

JOLT

awake,

half-

way

between dream

and smoke ...

Cross-modal storm.
Smell lightning before you see it. Ears
a rumbling afterthought.

———————

The ground's a rush
of adrenaline and exclamation
points. (Jousting

punctuation, neural-precision
voltage

... *touché!*)

Dry weather duel.
Loaded pistol sky.
Gunmetal. Combustible. An act of
Hell-ignition and heat-
demonic updraft. Noxious

whiff of wind and a thousand
tips-of-your-tongue
leaf their way downward. Stunned,

stunted. Terpene and ash …

———————

Cinders. Vocal stumps. (Dystonic.)

Ember-edged, tongue a slow-
burning
resignation.

Optic chiasma (sidewise perspective).

Look away: clouds are emission-fuelled,
cumuliform smokestacks (towers that won't

fall down ... *hush hush* ...).

———————

Smoke plumes. Pineal
convection. Folia blaze. (Cerebellar
volatility.)

———————

Caustic and sky
a drenched hammock.

Looming collapse; unravelling
fire, fibrous
nerve (stringy

precipitation). Look ...

Cross-
hatching

horizon. Mis-
fired
neurons. Criss-

acrostic blades
cut clear through rooftops,
telephone lines ... Trees

diagram the distance (point
A to points X),
so many burnings
at the stake. Sacrificial

lamp-
posts, hydro poles, wild-

fire raging.

Greyout.

Sky storied in fear.

(Yellow-bellied, sap-

sucking.) Sulphur

and pus, seething

dusk, all night

the scorching

song of cricket, Flaming

Tanager: Heat! Heat!

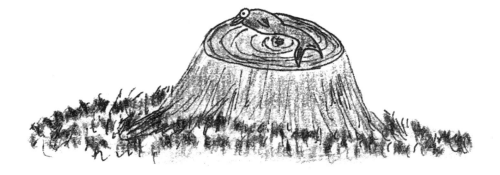

FISH/STUMP

GOING ...

53RD week forecast calls for intermittent anæsthetization. Thisaway, thataway. Anaptyctic sky. Not-quite-ice, not-quite-rain. Jello-visibility. The month between December and January teary with condensation. Supercooling droplets, howling window glass, the needle pitch of the small-voiced radiator.

Steam like an exhalation of old wounds. Carmine, rust, soggy bandages.
(Steam like a banshee.)

Somewhere in the room a glass of exposed nerves. Wisdom teeth tinkling like ice. *Jingle bells, jingle* … Xmas excavation. Xmas extraction. Your face smarts and what's left of your brilliance suctioned and spit down the drain. Gauze-packed. Frozen-jawed. Ceaseless chills and cold …

... compression; ice pick; an icicle between the eyes.

GOING ...

Concussive rhythm section: Crash cymbals. Ratchet. Thunder machine-headache.

And-a-one, and-a-two, and-a-three analgesics later ...

Quell the rain. Hell is your brain frozen over with too much reiteration. (Windows of nonstop bleeding. Elm trees of incessantly scraping fingernails.) Bad weather oozes into you unmediated. Wildly glandular. (A worsening ca-coughening!).

Endocrinic orchestra:

Flight of the wayward temporal lobe (*Is that God under your toque or are you just ecstatic
   to see me?*).
The well-tempered fornix (a brothel you can neither enter nor escape).
Amygdala amygdala amygdala (sensory overkill sends you anaphylactic).

Get out your handkerchief and undress

... your transorbital EpiPen.

SOURCES

The front epigraph by Derek Jarman is from *Chroma (A Book of Colour — June 1993)* (London: Vintage, 1995).

'Nerve Storms' — 'Nerve-storm' is a term coined by Edward Liveing, a Victorian neurologist, to characterize the explosive, unpredictable nature of migraines. Refer to Oliver Sacks's *Migraine* (Berkeley: University of California Press, 1992).

'Limbic swim' — 'Say! what a lot of fish there are' is from Dr Seuss's *One Fish, Two Fish, Red Fish, Blue Fish* (New York: Random House, 1960).

'Fishblood Sky' — The title 'Fishblood Sky' is derived from a line in 'North Winter,' a poem by Hayden Carruth in *Collected Longer Poems* (Port Townsend: Copper Canyon Press, 1994). The epigraph by Carruth in #9 of 'Fishblood Sky' is also from 'North Winter.'

'Cyclonic and whinnying' — The line 'Out in the sky, no one sleeps' in #2 is from Federico Garcia Lorca's poem 'Sleepless City,' in *Poet in New York*, translated by Greg Simon and Steven I. White, edited by Christopher Maurer (New York: The Noonday Press, 1998).

'Shifty Weather' — The Robert Kroetsch epigraph is from his poetry collection *The Hornbooks of Rita K.* (Edmonton: University of Alberta Press, 2001).

'Ravenousness' — The Rilke epigraph is from #2 of his 'Duino Elegies,' translated by Galway Kinnell and Hannah Liebmann in *The Essential Rilke* (New York: The Ecco Press, 2000).

'Strange Birds; Twitching Birds' — The epigraph in #4 by Robinson Jeffers is from his poem 'Birds and Fishes,' in *Rock and Hawk: A selection of shorter poems* (New York: Random House, 1987). Also in #4, the phrase 'Damn this cracked crow' is from Aristophanes's play *The Birds,* in *Three Comedies* (Ann Arbor: University of Michigan Press, 1969). Translated by William Arrowsmith.

'Birds (an apocalyptic poem?)' — Several of the subtitles are from various sources: 'an apocalyptic poem?' is a reference to Federico Fellini who described Alfred Hitchcock's film *The Birds* as 'an apocalyptic poem' (see Donald Spoto's *The Art of Alfred Hitchcock*, New York: Doubleday, 1979); 'Death, Judgement, Heaven, Hell,/and Spring,' is from Phyllis Webb's poem 'Eschatology of Spring' in *The Vision Tree: Selected Poems* (Vancouver: Talonbooks, 1982); 'marked by claws and cloudburst' is a phrase from Lorca's poem 'Sleepless City' in *Poet in New York*; and 'Five/jays/discuss/goodandevil' is from Hayden Carruth's 'North Winter.'

'Truncated' — The line by Yusef Komunyakaa is from his poem 'Shrines,' in *Pleasure Dome: New and Collected Poems* (Middletown, Connecticut: Wesleyan University Press, 2001).

ACKNOWLEDGEMENTS

Poems from *Nerve Squall* have previously been published or presented in the following periodicals and broadcasts:

'Nerve Storms' #s 1–8 in *Mid-American Review* (Fall 2001); #s 1–6 in *Contemporary Verse 2* (Winter 2001); #s 7 and 8 in *NeWest Review* (February 2001). 'Nerve Storms' was also published in Milieu Press's *Portfolio Anthology* (Vancouver, 2004).

'Limbic swim' in *Matrix* (Fall 2002).

'Fishblood Sky' in *The Malahat Review* (Summer 2001); broadcast on *Random Play*, CBC Radio 2 (July 2004) and on *Gallery*, CBC Radio Saskatchewan (April 2004).

'Into the Bizarro Squall' in *Matrix* (Fall 2002); broadcast on *Connecting*, CBC Radio 2 (July 2003) and on *Gallery*, CBC Radio Saskatchewan (March 2002).

'Agitated Sky Etiology' in *The Malahat Review* (Spring 2002).

'Shifty Weather' and 'Ravenousness' in *Contemporary Verse 2* (Fall 2002).

'Fishblood Sky' won *The Malahat Review*'s Long Poem Prize in 2001.

'Nerve Storms' was nominated by *Mid-American Review* for a 2001 Pushcart Prize.

'Agitated Sky Etiology' was nominated by *The Malahat Review* for a 2002 National Magazine Award.

'Birds (an apocalyptic poem?)' was a finalist for *The Fiddlehead*'s Ralph Gustafson Poetry Award in 2001.

NOTES FROM THE AUTHOR

For their support and encouragement, thank you many times over to Susan Andrews Grace, Kelley Jo Burke, Donna Hendrickson, Doris Larson, Tim Lilburn, Helen Marzolf, Liz Philips, Carla-marie Powers, Susan Shantz, Steven Ross Smith, Sue Stewart, Jennifer Still, Betsy Warland and an extra big thank you to my little buddy Leif Warland Shantz for appreciating goofiness all around ... My apologies to anyone I've forgotten.

Thank you to Tamara Bond for the fantastic original cover image.

I am grateful to the Saskatchewan Arts Board for funding that enabled me to work on this collection.

Thanks also to Kellogg's and Jet-Puffed, the combination of whose products coalesce into my favourite food group.

Nerve Squall is Sylvia Legris's third book-length poetry collection; her previous books are *iridium seeds* and *circuitry of veins*. She has twice been nominated for a Pushcart Prize, in 2001 she won the *Malahat Review*'s Long Poem Prize for 'Fishblood Sky,' and she received an Honourable Mention in the poetry category of the 2004 National Magazine Awards. She is currently a resident in the state of fidgety fretfulness.

Typeset in Bulmer.
Printed and bound at the Coach House on bpNichol Lane, 2005.

Designed by Bill Kennedy
Drawings by Sylvia Legris
Cover image by Tamara Bond

Coach House Books
401 Huron Street on bpNichol Lane
Toronto, Ontario   M5S 2G5

416 979 2217
800 367 6360

mail@chbooks.com
www.chbooks.com